Barbecue Cookbook

*Delicious Barbecue Recipes, Sauces, Rec~
And Ma~~*

Raymon

TERMS & CONDITIONS

TABLE OF CONTENTS

Chapter 1 – Barbecue Cookbook

Get ready for some really tasty barbecue recipes!!

Extraordinary Barbecue Chicken Breasts

A fine recipe, it just works.

ingredients

- 2 to 3 Tbsps Tomato Ketchup
- Zest Of 1 orange
- 1 to 1 1/4 tsp Sea Salt
- Freshly Ground Black Pepper To Taste
- 1 1/2 to 2 tsp Dijon or English Mustard
- 4 x 25 1 gram Skinless Chicken Breasts
- 2 to 3 tablespoons Honey
- 1 Dried Chilli
- 1 to 2 tsp Olive Oil
- 1 1/2 to 2 teaspoon (Heaped) Smoked Paprika

What to do

1. Assemble all the ingredients at one place.
2. In your bowl place the finely grated zest of the orange, along with the dried chili (crumbled), the paprika, mustard, honey, tomato ketchup and the olive oil. Then afterward combining all these ingredients together combine a pinch of salt along with pepper and then stir again.
3. Take out a couple of spoonful of the mixture made and place to one side. To the rest of the marinade in the bowl, please combine the chicken breasts.
4. Please turn them over, so they are completed coated by the marinade and then cover with plastic wrap before leaving to one side for 5 to 10 minutes.

5. Now we can proceed to the next most important step.

6. Once the barbecue has heat up correctly, you need to put the chicken on the grill but remember that before you do, please make it sure you lightly oil it.

7. When you put them on the grill, make sure the heat underneath isn't too high. If you notice the outer part of the chicken is starting to char quickly then move them to a perhaps cooler part of the barbecue and reduce the heat if possible.

8. You should be aiming to cook the chickens on every side for about 5-10 minutes, turning them every minute and basting

them with some more of the marinade left in the bowl.

9. You should only withdraw them from the heat when they have turned a golden brown and are cooked all the way through.

10. One thing remains to be done now.

11. The best way of testing is to see if they are cooked all the way through is to push a skewer in. Now if the juices that flow out are clear, then you know the chicken is correctly cooked.

12. Withdraw from heat, then place on clean plates and spoon few of the sauces you put apart earlier over them.

13. Go ahead and eat it up.

It is very easy and quick recipe. This one is one of my favorites.

Super Chicken Wraps

This is the king recipe out there.

Marinade:

- 1 to 2 cloves garlic, minced
- 2 to 3 teaspoons Italian seasoning
- 4 to 6 Tbsps olive oil
- 2 to 3 teaspoons lemon pepper

Caesar Dressing:

- 1/2 to 1 tsp Italian seasoning
- 1/2 to 1 tsp seasoned pepper
- 1 clove garlic (Minced)
- 1 carton sour cream
- 1 to 2 tbsps milk
- About 2 to 3 Tbsps of Parmesan cheese (freshly grated)
- 4 tortillas
- Large resealable freezer bag
- Parmesan cheese, freshly grated

- 1 boneless, skinless chicken breast
- Romaine lettuce (Chopped)

The method of preparation:

1. Assemble all the ingredients at one place.
2. Add marinade ingredients in a small bowl.
3. Put half the marinade in a large resealable bag; reserve the other half of marinade for basting on the grill.
4. Now we can go ahead to the next most important step.
5. Combine chicken to bag, toss and refrigerate 1 to 6 hours.
6. Drain and discard marinade.

<u>Grill:</u>

1. One thing remains to be done now.
2. Preheat grill to medium; place chicken breast on the grill.
3. Cooking for minutes, turn and cook around 15-20 more minutes or maybe until chicken is cooked through, basting with reserved marinade.
4. Remove cooked chicken and then cut into strips.
5. Now in your small bowl, while the chicken is cooking, add all Caesar dressing ingredients. Warm the flour tortillas. Layer chicken, lettuce, dressing and Parmesan cheese in tortillas.
6. Smell the aroma, and now serve.

Let's dive in…

Serves: 4

Duke BBQ Steak Marinade

I bet that you'll love it.

What you need:

- 3 to 5 tablespoon Worcestershire sauce
- 1 to 2 clove garlic (Minced)
- 3 to 4 tbsp. red wine vinegar salad dressing
- Salt and pepper to taste
- 1 cup barbecue sauce
- 1/4 cup steak sauce
- 1 to 2 tbsp. Mustard prepared
- 3 to 4 tbsp. Soy sauce

instructions:

1. Assemble all the ingredients at one place.
2. In your small bowl (nonporous), please add the soy sauce, barbecue sauce, steak sauce,

mustard, red wine vinegar salad dressing, Worcestershire sauce, garlic and salt and pepper to taste.

3. Smell the aroma and serve.

One of the best recipes out there.

Historic Grilled Balsamic Steak

I bet that you'll love it.

What you need

- 1 to 2 tablespoon Balsamic Vinegar
- 2 Gloves Garlic
- 125 ml Soy Sauce
- 1/4 to 1 tsp Hot Sauce
- 1 to 2 tablespoons Worcestershire Sauce
- 950-gram Sirloin Steak (Should be approximately an inch thick)
- 250 to 260 ml Water
- 1 to 2 tablespoon Dijon Mustard
- 1 small onion

What to do

1. Assemble all the ingredients at one place.

2. Please the steak either into a glass dish or may be a bag that's sealable. Now add the rest of the ingredients above in a bowl or maybe a jug and whisk thoroughly.
3. Now we can go ahead to the next most important step.
4. Once you have mixed all the ingredients together, you can then pour over the steak and leave to marinate for 1 and 2 hours.
5. When you are ready to cook the steak, you should get your barbecue heated up and cook it above a medium to high heat.
6. One thing remains to be done now.
7. When the barbecue is at the right temperature, you should

withdraw the steak from the marinade and put it on the grill cooking it on each side for between 5 and 7.

8. Any leftover marinade should be discarded and once the steak is cooked to the way you or your guests like it you can now remove it from the heat and serve.

9. Go ahead and eat it up.

Go for it!! Trust me.

Extraordinary Grilled Chipotle Chicken

This is the one recipe you should look for.

What you need

- 1 to 2 tablespoon chipotle chiles in adobo sauce (Chopped)
- 3 to 4 chicken breast halves, boneless and skinless
- 2 to 3 tablespoons onion, finely shredded
- 1/2 cup barbecue sauce

How to prepare:

1. Assemble all the ingredients at one place.
2. Preheat grill. In a small saucepan, combine barbecue sauce, onion, and chipotle chiles and mix well.

3. Heat and now keep warm till ready to grill, then brush mixture on chicken.

Grill:

1. One thing remains to be done now.
2. Put chicken on a charcoal grill five inches from medium-hot coals or may be on medium heat on a gas grill.
3. Grill about 5 to 10 minutes, basting chicken occasionally.
4. Turn chicken; cook 10-15 minutes more or maybe till chicken is done.
5. Now please bring the remaining sauce to a boil and serve with chicken.
6. Smell the aroma and now serve.

Servings: 4.

Make it quickly.

Historic Marinade

What do you think?

What you need:

- 1 lemon
- 1 to 2 clove crushed garlic
- 1/2 to 1 cup soy sauce
- 1/4 cup olive oil

The method of preparation:

1. Assemble all the ingredients at one place.
2. In your small bowl or may be cup, blend soy sauce, olive oil, lemon juice, and garlic up
3. Now pour over meat, and refrigerate for one hour.
4. Go ahead and eat it up.

Hard on your pocket so cheers!!

Mystical Grilled Steak With Whiskey & Dijon Sauce

I bet that you'll love it

ingredients

- 1 to 2 tsp Freshly chopped Thyme
- 2 to 3 tbsps Whiskey
- About 1/2 to 1 teaspoon of Freshly Ground Pepper (Approx)
- 1 to 2 Tbsps Light Brown Sugar
- ¼ to 1 tsp Salt
- 125 ml Reduced Sodium Beef or may be Chicken Broth
- 1 to 2 tsp Worcestershire Sauce
- 2 to 3 tbsps Dijon Mustard
- 455 Gram Skirt Steak
- 1 Large Shallot

What to do

1. Assemble all the ingredients at one place.
2. Preheat your barbecue to medium-high heat. While the barbecue is heating up, you can prepare the sauce. To do this, you need to combine in a saucepan the shallot, whiskey, mustard, brown sugar, thyme and Worcestershire sauce.
3. Bring all these ingredients to the boil then reduce the heat so that a lively simmer is maintained.
4. Now we can go ahead to the next most important step.
5. It is important you whisk this sauce frequently to prevent it sticking to the sides of the saucepan and burning. Keep it simmering for around 5-10

minutes or until it has been reduced down by about half. Then withdraw from the heat.

6. Now you need to cook the steaks on the barbecue. But before you do, please top both sides with the salt and pepper.

7. One thing remains to be done now.

8. Now if you want medium, you should probably cook each steak for 3 to 5 minutes on every side.

9. However, you should cook them for less time if you want yours to be medium (rare).

10. Once they've been cooked for the required amount of time, withdraw them from the grill and let them rest for six minutes before serving with the sauce.

11.   Smell the aroma, and now
you can serve.

Now the wait is over for hungry
people.

King sized Grilled Sesame Chicken

This is the king recipe out there.

Ingredients:

- 2 to 3 tablespoons sesame seeds
- 1/2 cup olive oil
- 1 to 2 teaspoon ground ginger
- 1/4 cup water
- 1/3 to 1 tsp red pepper
- 1/4 cup onion (Sliced)
- 1/2 to 1 cup soy sauce
- 2 cloves garlic (Minced)
- 1 to 2 tablespoon sugar
- 4 to 6 chicken breasts

Directions:

1. Assemble all the ingredients at one place.

2. In your medium bowl, mix, garlic, sugar, olive oil, water, sesame seeds, soy sauce, onion, ginger and red pepper.
3. Now we can go ahead to the next most important step.
4. Put chicken in a shallow container; add marinade just covering the chicken.
5. Now please reserve the marinade (remaining) for basting while you grill.
6. Marinate for 10 to 12 hours, turning chicken once; drain and discard marinade.
7. One thing remains to be done now.

Grill:

Grill chicken about 40-50 minutes or until done, basting with marinade occasionally.

Servings: 7-10

Sizzle your taste buds….

Typical Marinade (Carne Asada)

Wait, what is this?

Ingredients:

- Salt and pepper to taste
- 3 to 4 tbsp. Fresh lemon juice
- 1 to 2 cloves garlic (Finely sliced)
- 3/4 cup extra virgin olive oil

What to do:

1. Assemble all the ingredients at one place.
2. In your medium bowl, blend garlic, extra virgin olive oil, fresh lemon juice, salt, and pepper.
3. Now we can go ahead to the next most important step.
4. Place beef in the mixture.

5. One thing remains to be done now.

6. Rub mixture into the meat.

7. Now please cover the large or medium bowl and then allow beef to marinate in the refrigerator for at least 2 to 3 hours or so before grilling as desired.

8. Smell the aroma and now serve.

Always the upper hand…

Lovely Steak (Peppered Rib Eye)

When you're fantastic, this is best!!

ingredients

- 1 1/2 to 1 tsp Lemon Pepper Seasoning
- 1 to 2 tbsp Olive Oil
- 1 to 2 teaspoon Salt
- 1/2 to 1 teaspoon Cayenne Pepper
- 1 to 2 teaspoons Crushed Dried Thyme
- 4 x 285 to 340-gram Rib Eye Steaks
- 2 to 3 teaspoons Crushed Dried Oregano
- 1 to 2 tbsp Paprika
- 1 to 2 tbsp Garlic Powder

- About 1/2 to maybe 1 teaspoon of Freshly Ground Black Pepper

instructions

1. Assemble all the ingredients at one place.
2. Now please trim any excess fat from your steak and then please brush with olive oil.
3. Also, snip the edges of the steak before coating to prevent them curling up when grilling on the barbecue.
4. Now we can go ahead to the next most important step.
5. In your bowl blend the other ingredients together before topping over the meat evenly and also before rubbing it into the meat with your fingers.

6. Place on a clean plate and cover the steaks once both sides have been coated in the dry mixture before placing in a refrigerator for one hour.

7. One thing remains to be done now.

8. To cook the steaks withdraw from refrigerator while the barbecue is heating up and when ready cook them directly over a medium heat and cook until they are done to the way you want.

9. For steaks (medium rare) cook for between 10 to 20 minutes, turning them once. While if you want yours cooked to medium then now keep then on the grill for between 10-15 minutes.

Again turning them above once during this time.

10. Go ahead and eat it up.

One of the best recipes out there.

Supreme Baby Back Pork Ribs

Wow, just wow!!

What you need:

- 2 to 3 Tbsps. White sugar
- 2 to 3 Tbsps. Salt
- 2 to 3 Tbsps. Cider vinegar
- 1 to 2 Tbsps. Onion powder
- ¾ cup barbecue sauce
- 1 to 2 Tbsps. chili powder
- 1 to 2 tablespoon. fennel seed
- 3 to 4 Tbsps. paprika
- 1 to 2 tablespoon. Garlic powder
- 6 lbs. Pork baby back ribs
- 3 to 4 tsp. Ground black pepper
- 3 Tbsps. Honey

Instructions:

1. Assemble all the ingredients at one place.
2. Using a coffee grinder or maybe a blender, grind the fennel seed and salt together.
3. Shift the fennel and salt mixture in a mixing bowl, and stir together with onion powder, chili powder, garlic powder, black pepper, paprika, and sugar.
4. Divide the pork slab by slicing into three parts, having 5 ribs for every piece.
5. With a paper towel, pat dries the ribs and rub every piece with the spice mixture. Arrange the ribs on a large plate, and cover with a plastic wrap. Chill for about 8 hours.

6. Now we can go ahead to the next most important step.

7. Let ribs stand at ambient temperature for approximately 1 hour.

8. Prepare indirect grilling by preheating the smoker between temperatures of about 260 to 275°F arranging the charcoal briquettes on one side. Coat the grate lightly with oil.

9. Grill the ribs for approximately 1 to 2 hours with the grill's cover closed down.

10. While grilling, toss each rib once. Remove the ribs and set them away when each of their centers is no longer pinkish, or may be when the temperature inside its center registers about 150 to 160°F.

11.   One thing remains to be done now.

12.   In your small saucepan, combine and blend the cider vinegar, honey, and barbecue sauce.

13.   Bring the mixture to a boil; turn the heat low and simmer for approximately 15 to 25 minutes till the sauce is smooth and thickened. Brush every rib with the sauce.

14.   Grill back the ribs for a quarter of an hour on each side; turn each rib once and baste with the remaining sauce. Before serving, let the ribs sit for about 10 to 15 minutes.

15.   Smell the aroma and serve.

Time: 11 hours to 12 hours

Servings: 6 to 7

Not hard on your pocket so cheers!!

Mystical Turkey Marinade

Barbecue is the best.

What you need:

- 1 cup Creole seasoning
- 1/2 to 1 cup cayenne pepper
- 2 to 3 tablespoon. garlic powder
- 1 to 2 bottle Italian dressing
- 1/2 to 1 cup black pepper

What to do:

1. Assemble all the ingredients at one place.
2. In your medium bowl, mix Creole seasoning, 3/4 dressing (Italian), black pepper, cayenne pepper, and garlic powder.
3. One thing remains to be done now.

4. Rub above turkey, using leftover Italian dressing to fill the cavity.
5. Allow turkey to marinate for 6 to 8 hours, or overnight, before deep-frying as desired.
6. Go ahead and eat it up.

Go for it!! Trust me.

Cute Garlic & Herb Marinade

Sizzle your taste buds & get the taste of this simple yet tantalizing recipe.

What you need

- 1 to 3 tsp. poultry seasoning
- 12 to 14 cup vinegar
- 1 to 2 teaspoon. Salt
- 1 to 2 teaspoon. Ground black pepper
- 1 tsp. Dried thyme
- 11 to 14 cup water
- 1 to 2 teaspoon. dried Italian-style seasoning
- 13 cup vegetable oil
- 1 to 2 tsp. dried rosemary (Crushed)
- 2 to 3 cloves garlic (minced)

What to do

1. Assemble all the ingredients at one place.
2. In your medium bowl, blend the water, thyme, rosemary, Italian-style seasoning, poultry seasoning, vinegar, oil, garlic, salt and ground black pepper.
3. Now please blend it well and then apply it to your meat.
4. Smell the aroma and serve.

Stupidly simple…

Mystical Marinade (Fajita)

You know that I used to go to my amazing and awesome neighbor's house to eat this one. Completely free for me. Now what are friends for?

Ingredients:

- ¼ to 1 teaspoon. dried thyme
- 1 cup lemon juice
- 1 to 2 tablespoon. dried oregano
- 1 clove garlic (Minced)
- 1 to 2 cup vegetable oil
- 1 to 2 tbsp. shredded green onion
- 1/4 to 1 tsp. dried rosemary

Instructions:

1. Assemble all the ingredients at one place.
2. Now in your medium or maybe large bowl, please mixtogether

thyme, green onion, lemon juice, vegetable oil, rosemary, oregano and garlic up

3. One thing remains to be done now.
4. Put beef or chicken in the marinade.
5. Cover and marinate it in the refrigerator about 24 hours before grilling as desired.
6. Go ahead and eat it up.

Good luck!!

Supreme Steak Marinade

Oh yeah!!

Ingredients:

- 1 cube chicken bouillon (Crushed)
- 1/2 to 1 cup butter (Melted)
- 1 to 2 teaspoon. Greek seasoning
- 1 to 2 pinch of salt
- 1 pinch garlic powder

Instructions:

1. Assemble all the ingredients at one place.
2. Whisk the seasoning salt, seasoning (Greek), garlic powder, and bouillon cube into the melted butter.
3. Now we can proceed to the next most important step.

4. Mix until the bouillon cube melts.
5. One thing remains to be done now.
6. Now pour the marinade into a wide and shallow dish and place a steak of choice within the marinade, turning to coat both sides.
7. Cook or grill as desired.
8. Smell the aroma and serve.

Just make it once and you will keep making it!!

Cute Awesome Marinade

There are no words to express this recipe.

Ingredients:

- 1 clove garlic (Minced)
- 1 to 2 tbsp. toasted sesame seeds
- 1 pinch ground black pepper
- 1 green onion (Chopped)
- 5 to 6 tbsp. Soy sauce
- 2 to 3 tablespoon. White sugar
- 2 to 3 tablespoon. Sesame oil
- 1 to 2 tablespoon. All-Purpose flour

Instructions:

1. Assemble all the ingredients at one place.
2. Now in your large bowl, please mix the soy sauce, green onion,

ginger over high heat till well blended.

3. Now please let it boil and then reduce the heat to low and you may then cook for 10 to 15 minutes.

4. Now we can go ahead to the next most important step.

5. Take out the mixture from the heat then let it cool, and then crush well while slowly adding the lemon juice and hot chili paste.

6. One thing remains to be done now.

7. Put the chicken in the mixture and cover.

8. Store in the refrigerator at least 4 hours before preparing chicken as preferred.

9. Smell the aroma, and now you can serve.

The excellent recipe is just below!! Learn it by heart.

Legendary Grilling Marinade

If you're a legend, then make this one.

What you need:

- 1/2 to 1 tsp. lemon-pepper seasoning
- 1/2 to 1 tsp. Freshly ground black pepper
- 1 to 2 teaspoon. Kosher salt
- 1 to 2 tsp. hot pepper sauce
- 1 to 2 cup olive oil
- 4 to 6 cloves garlic, coarsely chopped
- 1 to 2 teaspoon. dried oregano flakes
- 1/2 cup minced yellow onion
- 1 cup freshly squeezed orange juice

- 1/2 cup freshly squeezed lime juice
- 1/4 to 1 cup shredded cilantro
- 1/2 to 1 teaspoon. ground cumin

What to do:

1. Assemble all the ingredients at one place.
2. In your blender, pulse the garlic & onion until it is very finely sliced.
3. Now we can proceed to the next most important step.
4. Now pour in orange juice, lime juice; season with cumin, oregano, salt, cilantro, lemon, pepper, black pepper and hot pepper sauce.
5. One thing remains to be done now.

6. Blend till thoroughly incorporated.
7. Now please pour in the olive oil and then blend until smooth.
8. Smell the aroma, and now you can serve.

You want to know what so special about this recipe. Why should I tell? Check it out for yourself.

Historic Mouth Watering Steak Tip Marinade

Yeah, it is a vintage recipe.

Ingredients:

- 2 to 3 tsp. garlic pepper seasoning
- 2 to 3 pounds beef sirloin tip steaks
- 1/2 to 1 cup Worcestershire sauce
- 1 cup Italian-style salad dressing
- 1 cup barbecue sauce

Instructions:

1. Assemble all the ingredients at one place.
2. Now in your large bowl, please mix the Worcestershire sauce,

salad dressing (Italian-style), garlic pepper seasoning and barbecue sauce as required.

3. Now please place the meat in the marinade and then please turn to coat.

4. Now we can proceed to the next most important step.

5. Now you may wrap, and then refrigerate it for at least one hour or so.

6. Preheat grill for high heat.

7. Brush grill lightly with oil to avoid sticking.

8. One thing remains to be done now.

9. Put steaks on the grill, and remove marinade.

10. Grill steaks for about 10-15 minutes on every side, or may be to the desired doneness.

11.	Smell the aroma and serve.

Now the wait is over for hungry people.

Stunning Garlic Grilling Marinade

Don't wait, eat it!!

What you need:

- 1 to 2 tbsp salt
- 2 to 4 teaspoon. Black pepper
- 1/2 cup olive oil
- 3 to 4 teaspoon. Crushed garlic

Instructions:

1. Assemble all the ingredients at one place.
2. Now in your blender or maybe food processor; please add garlic, salt, olive oil and pepper.
3. Process for about 10-15 minutes.
4. Go ahead and eat it up.

Extraordinary Simple Teriyaki Marinade

Be super

What you need:

- 1 clove garlic (Minced)
- 1 to 2 teaspoon. Ground black pepper
- 1/2 to 1 cup orange juice
- 1/2 to 1 cup soy sauce
- 1/4 cup packed brown sugar

The method of preparation:

1. Assemble all the ingredients at one place.
2. Now in your small or medium bowl, please stir together garlic, soy sauce, orange juice, brown sugar and pepper.
3. One thing remains to be done now.

4. Pour above beef, pork, or may be chicken.
5. Cover, and marinate it in the refrigerator for 4 hours, or maybe overnight.
6. Go ahead and eat it up.

Show time!!

Speed Marinade

Your friends and family are waiting. Hurry!!

What you need:

- 2 to 3 tbsp. Sesame seeds
- 1 to 2 cloves crushed garlic
- 2 to 3 tablespoon. lemon juice
- 1/3 to 1 cup Italian-style salad dressing
- 1/3 cup soy sauce
- 1 to 2 tsp. ground ginger

What to do:

1. Assemble all the ingredients at one place.
2. Now in your glass dish (nonporous) or maybe a bowl, please combine the lemon juice, sesame seeds, salad dressing, soy sauce, ginger and garlic.

3. One thing remains to be done now.
4. Blend it together properly.
5. Now please add favorite meat and then please marinate, cover it and refrigerated, for at least 2 hours or so.
6. Smell the aroma and serve.

There it is.

Super Vinegar Sauce (BBQ)

Ingredients:

- 1/2 to 1 tsp. cayenne pepper
- 1 to 2 tablespoon. brown sugar
- 1 to 2 cup cider vinegar
- 1/2 to 1 tablespoon. salt
- 1 to 2 tsp. crushed red pepper flakes

Instructions:

1. Assemble all the ingredients at one place.
2. Now in your medium bowl, please add the cayenne pepper, vinegar, salt, crushed red pepper flakes and brown sugar as required.

3. Blend it well and allow ingredients to mesh for about 4 to 8 hours before using.
4. Smell the aroma, and now you can serve.

Cute Speedy Marinade

What you need:

- 1/2 to 1 teaspoon. Worcestershire sauce
- 1/2 to 1 teaspoon. minced fresh ginger root
- 1 to 2 teaspoon. onion powder
- 1/2 to 1 tsp. garlic powder
- 1 to 2 teaspoon. smooth peanut butter
- 3 to 4 tbsp. soy sauce
- 1 teaspoon. corn syrup
- 2 to 3 tablespoon. barbecue sauce
- 2 to 3 teaspoon. black pepper
- 1 to 2 tbsp. vegetable oil
- 1 teaspoon. chili powder
- 1 to 2 tsp. white wine

Method of preparation:

1. Assemble all the ingredients at one place.
2. In your shallow dish, mix soy sauce, barbecue sauce, corn syrup, oil, wine, peanut butter, and Worcestershire sauce.
3. Now we can go ahead to the next most important step.
4. Season with black pepper, onion powder, ginger, chili powder, and garlic powder.
5. One thing remains to be done now.
6. Mix till it is smooth.
7. Marinate the meat for two to four hours.
8. Go ahead and eat it up.

Silently, you were waiting for this one. Don't lie…?

Thanks for reading my book.

Printed in Great Britain
by Amazon

36408524R00040